T0208181

Painted Over White

A Recurring Dream

Katie Abrams

authorHOUSE®

AuthorHouse™
1663 Liberty Drive
Bloomington, IN 47403
www.authorhouse.com
Phone: 1-800-839-8640

*Unless otherwise indicated, Scripture quotations used in this book
are from the Holy Bible, New International Version Copyright
© 1978 by New York International Bible Society.*

First published by AuthorHouse 4/7/2011

ISBN: 978-1-4567-5777-9 (e)
ISBN: 978-1-4567-5778-6 (sc)

Printed in the United States of America

*Any people depicted in stock imagery provided by Thinkstock are models,
and such images are being used for illustrative purposes only.
Certain stock imagery © Thinkstock.*

This book is printed on acid-free paper.

To others like me who call themselves seekers.

One night I had a disturbing dream about sitting down and spinning around with my arms stretched out side to side. Four days later I left extra early for work to avoid the traffic. It had rained the night before, and my husband cautioned me to be careful since the roads were slippery. As I entered the off-ramp for my exit, I took my foot off the accelerator. Halfway up the ramp my car started spinning out of control. I had no idea what to do other than scream in terror and amazement at the reality that I was experiencing the exact sensation I had dreamed about just a few days before. When the car stopped, a man in another car was stopped about twelve feet behind me with eyes as big as silver dollars and his mouth gaped open. I collected myself, straightened out the car and drove the remaining mile or so to work.

The story in this book is similar yet on a much larger scale. It was difficult to write; however, I hope you will hang in there with me to the end. I have included as many of the details I believe you need to understand the beginning, middle and end of an _extraordinary_ _supernatural_ _production_ that occurred in my life, without all the excess baggage of self-indulgence and monotony.

I am grateful to my husband, a "knight in shining armor" if there ever was one. God bless you, sweetheart.

Contents

1 – The Dream

People say they dreamed a dream or had a vision. The dreamer is somehow changed because of the stunning and sudden impact of the images upon his or her senses. What makes the dream or vision powerfully unique is that it does not coincide with the events from that day. You listen as they describe the details of the dream or vision, and you know from the telling that this was no ordinary occurrence. The images are forged deeply into the dreamer's conscience and are rarely if ever forgotten. The details are so intrinsically fresh, intact and easily recalled that it is difficult to categorize the event as a dream. Since most dreams are never remembered or quickly forgotten, the episode is not simply a dream but is transformed into a memory.

Dreams and visions are not defined the same way even

though the terms are used intermittently. A dream is defined as a series of thoughts, images or emotions occurring during sleep. On the other hand, a vision is defined as something seen in a dream, trance or ecstasy, or a supernatural appearance that conveys a revelation. The paranormal community refers to certain visions or dreams as premonitions. Visions and premonitions seem to fit naturally in the paranormal category due to the mystical connotations provided by the definitions. There are countless books, articles and personal accounts of exceptional visions experienced by people all over the world for thousands of years. These premonitions are helpful when the notice or warning is heeded and a powerful tool for those who seek to help themselves, their families and friends, or even mankind.

Are visions and premonitions evil? I tend to disagree. The words "dream" and "vision" are used collectively over 140 times in the Bible. Throughout the Old and New Testaments God communicates to men and women through dreams and visions. This is comforting to know. Since God is the same yesterday, today and tomorrow (Hebrews 13:8), I like the thought of God talking to us today the same way He did long ago and will continue to do so in the future.

What about recurring dreams? Imagine having the same dream over and over, year after year but not night after night, and never with any warning or clue from the day's events that the uninvited rerun will appear. It is preposterous to have the same dream every night, so the elusive device of the recurring dream is to use a hit-or-miss schedule to catch you unaware and unprepared. Is a recurring dream another type of premonition? Are premonitions gifts or curses, and are such episodes as fanciful as the wind? I cannot answer these questions authoritatively or venture any reliable guesses, especially with respect to recurring dreams. I can tell you, however, that it happened to me.

I experienced a recurring dream for 34 years. I shouldn't say experienced; I should say taunted, cursed or plagued. At least that is how I felt about it until the day the dream became a reality. On that particular day, I walked the walk, saw the sights, smelled the smells, heard the sounds, understood the feelings, and learned the dark secret. My curse became my gift and my greatest comfort. That day I resolved to transform myself from what I had become into the person I was meant to be.

I had a lot of love in my life, but my childhood was peppered with sleazy, tawdry experiences. I was neglected in ways that makes my skin crawl when I think about it now. My mother suffered child abuse and anti-Semitic persecution as a child. She was a kind person and would never intentionally hurt anyone; but when one of her flashbacks set upon her, she would act out her neurotic, avenging anger on me. Zero to Three, an organization devoted to childhood development research, states it is an inescapable conclusion that early childhood experiences have a lasting impact on our lives. I agree based on my case.

My first childhood memory is delightful. We were in my grandmother's house after church on Sunday. At some point I walked over to the piano and started pecking out a song. I heard my sister screaming, "Mama, Mama, come here, come here quick! The baby's playing the piano! She's playing the song from church!" She ran off screaming throughout the house and then outside. I continued to play as the havoc exploded around me. Everyone gathered around me, laughing and praising my accomplishment as I continued to peck out the song. I heard them, but the song in my head was louder and drowned them out. The song filled me up almost to the point of bursting, and I could feel it leave me as it drained through my fingers as I played. I had never experienced such an incredible emotion. I didn't know it then, but today I know that the emotion I was feeling was pure joy. Daddy grabbed me and held me high over his head as he giggled and tossed me up and down. He set me back on the bench to play, but the spell was broken, the song was gone, and I couldn't play it anymore. I was two years old.

I rode the wave of joy and accomplishment from that experience until I was molested at the age of three. A babysitter decided, I suppose for the sake of science and humanity, that it was necessary to pull down my pants and conduct a hands-on examination. I remember being on my back with my legs wide open looking at the ceiling and the walls. I never looked at the person, but I remember what was said. I did not like the spreading and the probing. I was confused. I felt so strange. When the episode was over, I was ordered to pull up my pants and swiftly sworn to secrecy or, "there's gonna be big trouble." The threat scared me so much that I never told a single soul, until now.

Sometime after that happened I was playing one afternoon with a little girl the same age as me - three. We were playing on the couch at her house down the street from where I lived. The mother was in the room busy sewing at the dining room table with her back to us. I remember the contrast of her long brown hair hanging down, covering her back and most of her light-colored shirt. Each time her little brother came over to try to play with us, I shoved him away. He was all wide-eyed and smiling. He couldn't have been more than 18 months old. He had to wear a helmet on his head, and I was told it was for his protection. I didn't care. I felt good when I shoved him. My last push was the hardest. He fell down and let out a blood-curdling scream.

The mother slammed her hands down, shot up from the table and stormed over to me. Her red-face glowed as her cheeks pulsed between her deep breaths. Her eyes were bulging and the tears streamed down her face. She was scary looking. I thought she was going to rip my head off. She screamed at the top of her voice, "Get out! You, you, get out of my house!" The father appeared out of nowhere and escorted me home. He told my mother what I had done and that I could never play with his children again. I was no good. I didn't know what was so horrible. The kid fell down and started crying. Big deal. It happened to me all the time, but nobody got all shook up about it.

I was not treated at home as though I had the plague or anything, but the news about that incident must have traveled fast. I was not welcome to play anywhere else. For a while I had no one to play with. One day some strange children arrived at our house. We played nicely up to the point my mother hauled me off to the bathroom to spank me for not sharing my toys. She said if I didn't share my toys with the other children that I would be spanked again "good and proper" and that I would not be allowed to play anymore. It was not long until I was dragged back into the bathroom for another spanking. Mama isolated me from the other kids until they were picked up. I cried so hard. I didn't understand sharing and why I had to be by myself. We moved to some apartments in a different county at some point. My parents had been planning to move for months, but I didn't know that aspect of the situation. I believed we had to move because of me, because I was no good.

I was molested again when I was about four years old by a little playmate. She pulled me behind the couch at her house and taught me all about masturbation. There were two older boys kneeling or standing on the couch and looking down at us, laughing and pointing. The little girl stopped and told me I had to stop, too. That was difficult because I was starting to like it. The boys kept laughing and heckling us. She said, "We shouldn't be doin' this … don't tell anybody about what we've been doin' or you're gonna get it!" I knew exactly what that meant. Another threat even scarier than the first one. They kept saying, "You're gonna get it, you're gonna get it!" I was feeling pretty good there for a while, but now I felt so horrible and dirty. I hated feeling that way. I don't remember ever seeing or playing with her again after that day.

There was an older boy who lived in our apartment complex. I played with him one time. He took three of us little girls aside to play his favorite game. The object of the game was to find out who was brave enough to lift their shirts for the pirate's "titty cutters" initiation ceremony. He took his knife and circled each of our breasts. We were members if we didn't flinch or cry. Something happened to that kid. I don't know what, but he just vanished one day.

We didn't live in that apartment complex very long. We moved again. This was our second move in about two years. My brother and sister were starting to act up and explore the drug scene. I found solace in the private joy of self-exploration. My mother must have seen me one day. She yelled at me, "Only filthy, disgusting trash does that.

No man will ever be able to satisfy you." I was four years old; I had no idea what she was talking about. I felt even more worthless and filthy than ever before. I felt so bad that I stopped bathing; mother had to force me.

I remember playing outside one day and one little boy about my age drew an outline of an anatomically correct lady in the sandbox, laid on top of her and began to perform how babies are made. Maybe my mother saw that from the window? I can't say. We soon moved again, but this time to a house.

I am sure that I had many happy and safe experiences as a small child. However, aside from the events I've just described, I don't remember much of anything else until a particular day soon after my fifth birthday. I experienced the first of what turned out to be a recurring dream. The day proceeded as usual as far as I know. I don't remember any traumatic event that had happened during the day. I believe that I ended up in my bed ready to go to sleep as always. Since no one ever read to me, I did not hear a scary bedtime story. To the best of my knowledge, my brother and sister had not picked on me that day. Nonetheless, that particular night I dreamed a certain dream.

I dreamed about a place.

I enter the place with no fear even though it seems strange to me. I enter through a door from the outside, yet I feel like I have been inside all the time as though the place surrounded me when I first saw it.

The place seems to be a room within a building yet there is no outside. As I walk through it, I cannot see the floor even though I look down. No matter where I look, my gaze cannot peer below a certain point as though someone is holding up a big black sheet blocking my vision as they move along with me, but I am totally alone. This frustrates me because I think that I should be able to see the floor. There is no mist or fog to obscure my vision, but my eyes just see black anytime I look down.

There are one or two turns as I make my way slowly, and I keep my arm extended out in front of me as I move along. I am starting to feel a little scared now. There is a strong, tangy-sweet odor in the place layered with a musty smell. There is a constant sound. It is a humming sound. It is not the humming sound from a person. This humming is distant and sounds like an engine or machine, and it is all around me now. There is a big window ahead of me, and then more big windows appear as I turn and look to the left. I counted six windows in all. They are side-by-side and bright, but I can't make out the shape of the windows. I look in other directions, but I see only a shadowy darkness. Nothing jumps out at me, yet I start to get very anxious.

Aside from the big windows, there are two prominent details. The first detail is the light. It is a singular, bright light that appears overhead and off to my right. The light is definitely above me, and it is hard to determine whether the light is outside or inside the place. It seems kind of high, and I cannot make out if the light is attached to something or freestanding. The light is not real high, but I do have to look up to see it. The light is very bright, but I have the feeling that it should be brighter. My heart starts to pound.

The most disturbing detail is the unusual color of the place. It is green. Everywhere is green. It is an unusual, indescribable and particular color of green. I know that I've never seen it before. It is not quite green or yellow or blue, but I know that it is definitely green. I am afraid of the color. I start focusing on the color. There are no people or animals to distract me, and nothing major happens. I don't see anything that should scare me, but the color scares me. As I start to focus on the color, I am horrified. I wake up.

My sister and I shared the same room, but we had separate twin beds. I stayed still to see if I woke her up, but she was sound asleep. I bargained with myself for a while whether to wake up my sister or my parents. I fell back asleep in the meantime.

The dream really disturbed me. It was so real that I could taste it. I told my mother about it the next morning. She shrugged me off saying that it was probably my first dream, and that I should try to forget it because everybody dreams. Forget it! Sounds easy, but it was quite impossible for me at the time. I was old enough to know that this was different from my other dreams because of how it affected me. It was all so vivid. I was sure that I had actually visited an unknown place. I was sad to think people had such horrible dreams all the time.

2 – Living with the Dream

I can't pinpoint the exact span of time between the first occurrence of this strange dream and the second one, but my guess is six to eight months. I arrived at this time frame based on my age of five at the time of the first dream, and the fact that I started school in the fall following my sixth birthday. I had the second dream shortly before the first day of school. The details of the dream unfolded exactly as presented in the first dream. It was uncanny, and it freaked me out.

I told my mother about it again, but she kept harping about how much I would love school and bought me some new clothes from the thrift store to get me excited. I started displaying a nervous tension, or angst, from the time I woke up in the morning until bedtime. Mother said I was just nervous about starting school and told me to settle down as the first day of school was "just around the corner."

When the first day finally arrived, I couldn't reconcile my mother's excitement with my anxiety. I was so nervous, and Mama could tell. She said not to worry, because she would take me to school. My mother held my hand the whole long way to the new elementary school (we lived across the street). I think we walked all of 80 yards right into the classroom.

I stopped dead in my tracks. Mama dragged me a little as she kept walking towards the teacher. I could not move. I heard her asking what was wrong with me. I must have been standing there with my mouth open. Mama started to scold me for being rude to the teacher, who by now had come over to us and was standing in front of me. They didn't see what I saw.

The walls were green. Then I noticed a disgusting smell. Yes, something was definitely wrong. I didn't say anything. I was frozen as my eyes traced around the room in the same pattern as in the dream. I started by looking up at the lights. There were bright lights overhead. Then I looked to the left and saw windows. I was gripped with fear and sure something terrible was going to happen to me. Naturally, my mother and the teacher assured me that I would be okay, and I was going to have so much fun learning and making new friends. Mama made excuses for my behavior saying that I had never acted like that before. They decided it was best to put me in the front row next to the teacher so she could watch me. The teacher told Mama she should stay for a while, so she sat in the back of the classroom.

I don't remember what we did in class that first day. I was too preoccupied with investigating my surroundings to see if this was the place in my dream. Almost everything was there -- the room was green, the windows, the lights, the smell -- but nothing matched up exactly. The green color was very close, but it was not the same color in my dream. I was looking for a certain green. The classroom was painted a vomit-green color. It was very, very close but still not the same. The lights were bright and hit me with the same impact, but there were too many of them. I was looking for a single, bright light that appeared to be capable of being brighter.

The windows were side-by-side up close to the ceiling. The windows in my dream were different somehow and there were less of them. The classroom had eight square windows. There were only six windows in the dream, and there was a certain distinction about them that I could not decipher. I just knew they scared me. I noticed a metal ring at the top center of each classroom window. The teacher used a long stick with a little metal hook-type deal attached at the end to reach up and pull or push the windows open or closed. Each window had an arm that slid up and down in a metal channel, and the arm was exposed when the window was in the open position. The windows in my dream were never open and had no metal ring at the top.

I was fixated on my dream and how these new surroundings were so very close. I didn't calm down. Does anyone know at age five what is happening in their subconscious in the wake of trauma? I surely did not. I didn't realize what was happening to me. My mind was setting up a defense system, an invisible force field or shield that surrounded me from the inside out. The system was created so fast that I didn't know it had happened and remained with me all my life, getting stronger and stronger with every insult and humiliation.

As my mind's defense mechanism was forming unbeknownst to me, I kept thinking about the details from the dream that were missing in the room. The smell was overpowering, but it wasn't the same smell in my dream. It must have been disinfectant. I noticed there was no humming sound. No humming. I felt good about that, so I took the next big step. I looked down.

I could look down! I could look down, and I could see something. I saw the tile floor. I saw the legs of my desk and chair. I saw my dress, my knees, my legs and socks and shoes. I saw the socks and shoes of the other children around me. I could see the bottom of the teacher's dress, her legs, her shoes and the base of the podium in front of her. I could look down, and I could see things. I could look around and see everything in the classroom. I saw all of the other children, the blackboards, the decorations on the walls, the coat rack, and the other mothers in the back of the room sitting with my mother. There was no black curtain and no shadowy darkness.

On the way home Mama asked me if I felt better about school. That was hard to answer because I didn't really pay attention to what the teacher had to say. She didn't know that I was preoccupied with examining my surroundings and comparing them to the details of the dream. The walls were certainly green, the room smelled, and there were lights above me, the windows, everything. There was so much detail that was similar and yet so different. I knew this was not the place in my dream. The shade of green was very close, but it was off. I couldn't decide if it was too dark or too light, but it wasn't the same color. The light in my dream was a bright light over my head but off to the right, not a series of overhead lights. The windows were scary because they looked so close to the windows in the dream but yet they were so very different. The most familiar thing about the windows was the good amount of daylight that shown through them. This made them seem friendly and unimposing.

The dream occurred often. The timing was always elusive, and I never dreamed the dream two nights consecutively.

The dream was always exactly the same in every detail. I wanted desperately to get my mother to help me. I was afraid to tell anyone else. I loved my mother so dearly. If she couldn't help me, no one could. She was such a beautiful woman and just being around her made me happy. We would watch old movies together at home all the time. She loved the old movies. She wanted desperately to be a movie star herself. She had the looks but no talent, plus she couldn't read. She took me with her to the movie theater anytime she had the money to go. We saw tons of movies. Except for foreign movies, I don't think there is a movie made I have not watched at least once. Mystery stories quickly became my favorite genre. I loved it when the crime was solved and the bad guy was exposed and brought to justice. I wanted that so much for myself.

I was so anxious during my elementary school years every time I entered a new classroom. The rooms were always painted a hideous color of green (what I always referred to as vomit green), even when I switched schools in the fourth grade. By the time I got to the eighth or ninth grade, most all of the rooms were painted brownish-tan or beige color; and, best of all, the classrooms had central heating and air conditioning so no more big windows.

The lights were laid out generally in a series of long, fluorescent overhead canisters. Once when I was in sixth grade, I was at school after dark for some function. I remember turning a corner and seeing a singular light that stopped me in my tracks. I stood there, stared at it, conjured up the light from my dream, and then compared the two. The similarity was very close, but it was not the light in my dream.

I stopped trying to discuss the dream with my mother as my early teens rolled around. It was an exercise in futility since nothing ever came of it other than perplexity and annoyance. Mama was very sensitive in the area of extra-sensory perception and psychic phenomena. She was mildly sympathetic as to how the dream affected me. She didn't know any of my other secrets, so she probably decided that the dream was all that was eating at me. She revealed some of her psychic experiences and tried to help me figure out what the dream represented.

I asked her to tell me about myself and what my life was like from birth to age five. She laughed. She told me that I would wrap myself around her leg and hang on so tight she had to drag me around with her wherever she went. My brother and sister hated it. They kept telling her, "Mama, make her stop," but she said to leave me alone. I sucked a pacifier and a bottle until I turned six. Ah! I remembered instantly after she said it. I recalled her gently guilting me into giving up my "pup" and "babbas." She said, "You're going to be in school soon, and none of the other children will be sucking a pup or drinking a bottle. You can quit for your sixth birthday, and then you won't miss them when you start school." She said my grandparents used to fight over who got to hold me. They used to pull on me like a wishbone until my father had to break them up for fear one of them would rip my arm off. She told me about the time she spanked me for not sharing my toys with some children she was babysitting at the time. I told her that I remembered that incident. She got offended and thought I believed that she ruined me because she spanked me. She said in her defense, "Be glad I didn't throw knives at you like my mother did to me." I had heard enough at that point; I never asked her about it again.

Mother also described how she felt that one time when I played the piano at my grandmother's house. She always made sure we had a musical instrument in the house when they could afford it. We had a little organ in the apartment. I don't remember how or when we got it, or if it had always been with us. The organ was like an ashtray to me. My parents must have wanted to have it handy in case one of their friends or neighbors could play.

I was not encouraged to play or forced to take lessons; my mother preferred to use guilt. She always said, "You should learn how to play the piano so you can be the life of the party and people will like you." She thought that I wanted to be the center of attention like she always needed to be. I abhorred the idea of calling attention to myself.

Mother knew the chords for part of one or two classic songs, and she loved playing a little boogie-woogie music every now and then.

One day I sat down at the organ and began to play "Ebb Tide", a popular song at the time. I had heard it so much on the radio and television that I could play the whole song by ear, melody and chords with both hands. My mother was flabbergasted and thrilled. I think I played the song once for Daddy and maybe a couple of times after that and then stopped.

The dream, however, kept pestering me year after year. That's all I could think about. I developed a bad skin condition around the age of 10. I had to soak in a stinky solution. It smelled like sulphur. There was also a cream that Mama rubbed all over me before I went to bed. The doctor could not provide any clue as to what caused the outbreaks and assured us that the combination of soaks and salves would work. The doctor hinted that I might be suffering from a nervous condition but stopped short of recommending a psychological evaluation, probably because he knew we were poor. He assured Mama that my skin would clear up, but it didn't. The condition stayed with me for years.

The doctor didn't know that my mother was a hopeless neurotic and herself a victim of sexual abuse and hate crimes. She used to have flashbacks and act out at me, unfortunately.

My father was at work so I was stuck with her until the arrival of a blessed distraction. I never knew what set her off when she would have a flashback and start yelling it out with whoever had harmed her. Her tantrums were bad enough, but she always screamed hysterically at me, acting out all the parts while screaming and crying in my face. I was so young when it started and continued until I got old enough to figure out I didn't have to stand there and take it. I think I was twelve years old. It was such a weird part of my life. I never knew what to do but just stand there. Her stories were hideous and gut wrenching. She suffered in shocking ways, and I wanted so much to be able to comfort her. She would always snap out of it if the phone rang or eventually wind down on her own. No matter what, however, she always knew when Daddy would get home from work and how long it would take her to pull herself together.

I was rather preoccupied with my experiences plus I was harboring my mother's baggage as well. There was always a committee meeting going on in my head as a result. I developed strange little habits. I kept making the same noise all the time. It sounded like I was saying "gully gully" over and over. As I got older I counted out syllables on my fingers while I was thinking, or talking or reading. Counting preoccupied me. I would count one through eight real fast, over and over. If I wasn't counting, I was clicking beats. With my tongue, I would click the beat from a song on the roof of my mouth. I constantly tapped my fingers, and I bit my fingernails. I sucked on a finger, not my thumb. In my mind, thumb sucking was a clear signal that you had a problem. I hummed all the time. When I got old enough to take showers, I would sing at the top of my voice until the water turned cold. It's funny; I never got in trouble for wasting all that water.

My brother and sister dropped out of school and moved out on their own to join the hippie and drug cultures. My brother was in and out of jail all the time. I could hear my parents whimpering in their room about how they lost their kids. Naturally I assumed I was included in the tally. Mama had less to do which turned out to be a bad thing. She did not handle the empty-nest syndrome well at all. She tried to remodel the house, but she didn't have a clue how to go about it. She had champagne taste with a beer pocketbook. She just kept adding a lot of cheap junk to each room. The house basically ended up looking like a thrift store. Daddy installed gold shag carpet throughout the house, except I got hot pink shag carpet in my room. The master bedroom was red velvet from head to toe, except for the walls.

I was in school when Daddy started painting the walls. I could smell the paint as soon as I walked through the door. The small entry walls were paneled with wood on one side and covered with mirrors on the other. It wasn't until I got about ten feet into the house and stepped into the living room that I saw the color. I dropped my stuff and fell to my knees. My father ran over to me and called for Mama. I know they said words to me, but I couldn't hear them. I finally answered, correction, shouted:

"Green? You had to pick green?"

Mama answered, "It's Avocado Green. Well that's how the professional decorator lady down the street painted her house, so it must be right."

Right. Green. I was numb for a while. I quickly dismissed the color from that of my dream, but I was nonetheless affected. I went through all the motions, responded correctly, did well in school, won awards, played well with others, etc. I did all the things a good kid is supposed to do, but I don't remember any of it. I saw photographs with me in them, alone or with others, but I can't tell you the circumstances or describe how I felt at the time the pictures were taken. I keep one special picture taken of me with my best friend. We were fifth graders at the time. In the picture we are both laughing while she's holding me up. I remember everything about that picture, who took it, what happened before and after, how I felt, what the weather was like, and how the day ended. That one picture represents my childhood to me. I have thrown all the other pictures away.

As I approached 15, the dream's appearance became a habit and less frightening. I noticed that my skin condition began to subside as I got more comfortable with the dream itself. I never welcomed the dream as a friend or anything; but since nothing truly horrible ever happened, I resolved that I was a freak and this was something that I had to deal with alone. The strange green color, the bright light, and the big windows became like billboards to me. When I saw a familiar billboard, I just recognized it and went about my business.

I noticed that as I got older, it was easier to "call up" and review the dream. If I entered a room and it was green, I had to stop. I could settle down and proceed after I reviewed and confirmed in my mind that it was not the same color as the green in my dream. I attended several outdoor, nighttime activities where there were bright lights all over the place. Although a light may have been above me or attached to a roof, building or tree, I calmed down once I decided that the lights were very similar but not the same light in my dream.

There were occasions when I actually wanted to have the dream again so I could be sure about details; but I soon learned that my recurring dream had a schedule of its own, and I had to accept it as part of my life. I concluded that the dream was a sign that my overall school experience was going to be bad even though it didn't work out that way. I loved school and all of its opportunities. I made dear friends in school. I never told a soul about my recurring dream. I was too ashamed and embarrassed and figured they would think of me as a freak or making up a story to be "special." No one knew except my mother. I hadn't said anything to her about it for so long that I'm sure she put it out of her mind completely. She had enough of her own problems.

My high school counselor found a secretarial job for me during the summer break between my junior and senior years. While I longed for lazy days at the beach, I needed the money. I worked in a big office, and everyone worked at making me feel welcome. Toward the end of the summer, there was a baby shower for one of the secretaries. We didn't get much work done that day after the party. Everyone blew off the rest of the afternoon and started to leave early. I stayed behind to finish my typing assignment. I noticed a few of the other employees hung around also.

There was one particular fellow that was very nice to me. We joked around and laughed a lot. He was hanging around my desk and asked me to go with him to his office so we could talk. Soon after we got there, he locked the door and started coming on to me. I made some innocuous comment about having to get home to help my mother with supper and stepped toward the door. He lunged at me and grabbed me and put his hand over my mouth. There were no windows around the door of his office. He began to breathe heavy and pulled me behind his desk.

He kept trying to kiss me while keeping a tight clamp on my hair and neck. His grasp got tighter and more painful as I tried to get away from him. He stopped kissing on me and kept a tight grip on my neck with one hand as he unbuckled his belt and unzipped his pants with the other hand. The pants fell to his ankles as he stood up and yanked me onto my knees. The pungent smell of his oily skin and lack of personal hygiene made me gag. "Don't worry," he giggled, "women are always amazed when they see it." He forced my head down on him. I struggled and choked as I punched and scratched, trying to hurt him, but he laughed and said that it felt good. I leaned over and vomited when it was over.

I was silent as I made the short way down the hall to the elevator. I mulled over what happened knowing there was no way I could tell my parents about it. Mother would be hysterical and act like it had happened to her instead of me. My father would kill him. I dare not tell the police. I felt every ounce of empathy or sympathy for humankind drain from me as I drove home. I thought I better look at myself in the rear-view mirror and fix myself up before I go inside. I saw my face but my mouth was invisible. The whole episode was summarily buried with all my other secrets and humiliations. I carried on as though nothing had happened, yet I was changed forever. The blow to my psyche was significant. I didn't know it then but a significantly strong self-defense system guarding my emotions was altered to something so impervious that afternoon that I simply became incapable of any deep, guttural feelings. I think I can explain what happened to me, rather to my mind at this critical juncture. Imagine yourself in my place:

> I am sitting in a chair in the middle of a bright room. My forearms with my hands open and faced down are resting on the top of my thighs. The floor is carpeted, and all of the walls and the ceiling are covered with mirrors. My eyes are open, and I'm resting comfortably. All of the sudden, there is an impact from inside the room -- a silent sonic boom -- that causes a swift breeze to pass across my face. I close my eyes instantly before the glass starts blasting off the walls and ceiling. Glass and dust are flying everywhere in all directions at once. I keep my eyes shut real tight. I feel little points of pain as the glass cyclone swirls around me hitting my head, face, neck, shoulders, arms, and hands. The glass keeps falling all around me for what seems like forever in deafening crashes. The last little bit of glass finally falls in the corners and along the sides, and I hear the little tinkling from the back corner signaling that the devastation is over. I bow my head and open my eyes. I can see my chest, belly, arms, hands, and the carpet all around me covered in glass and dust. I lift up my hands and marvel at the clean outline of my arms and hands on the top of

my pants. Then I raise my head up and look around me. The room is just as it was before the shattering. Someone or something had hit the mirrors without breaking the glass. I see my reflection. I know I should be covered in glass, yet I am clean. I get up and walk out of the room.

3 – The Dream Investigated

Until this point in my life, I tried hard to fit in somewhere. I found out quickly as a kid that if I could make people laugh, then I could thwart potential attackers and they were less likely to pick on me. Because of my small size and inability to speak up for myself, I was vulnerable to bullying and oftentimes a target from girls I considered friends. Now, after what I felt was a severe violation, I felt completely worthless. I didn't care if I lived or died. I would pray at night to God for Him to kill me in my sleep. I spent a lot of time trying to figure out what I had done that was so awful. I turned into an Ice Princess. Nothing fazed me. I didn't cry at weddings or funerals. I didn't care who got married or had babies. I recall once when I was at work, something happened to cause the girls in the office to tear up. One gal was crying, and I remember saying she should stop. She glared at me in astonishment.

"What's your problem?", I asked her.

"My problem! You're the one with the problem. You're just standing there. How can you be so cold! I bet you wouldn't cry if your dog died!"

As I turned to leave the room, I heard everyone congratulating her for calling me out. She was right. I had become so hardened and so tough that I was unable to care, or at least let anyone know that I cared. I thought enough about myself to eat and keep clean. I liked nice clothes and always tried to be presentable. I was never forced to clean my room or the house. I never ironed anything, and my clothes were always wrinkled. My friend's mother knew something was wrong with me, and she always went out of her way to try to make me feel special. I had a couple of boyfriends that I thought I loved. I spent most of my time amazed that they were interested in me at all.

After I turned 15, the frequency of the recurrent dream toned down dramatically. I had the dream maybe once or twice a year and always in the fall before the holidays. The dream actually startled me when it occurred. Nothing changed at our house except Mama. Her personality changed dramatically. She lost interest in basic things and then went hog-wild in other areas. She couldn't or wouldn't keep up with the housework so much so that the dust on

all the tchotchkes caused her to develop serious allergies. Her dementia and hoarding had met at the fork in the road and embraced each other wholeheartedly. Daddy couldn't do anything about it. Anytime he started to move things around or clear junk out, she flew into hysterics. He had quietly resigned himself to her lifestyle after a few years of arduous battle.

I met the love of my life at age 18. Truly for us it was love at first sight. We were strangers who happened to be at a park on a certain Sunday afternoon. I made the mistake of introducing him to my parents. My guy simply did not measure up to my parents' standards and expectations for their future son-in-law. They expected me to marry a doctor or a lawyer. He was five years older than me, had a small child, and was in the first week of what would turn out to be a gruesome divorce. All of my life, my father never failed to caution me, "If you sleep with dogs, you are bound to get fleas." In other words, don't get involved with a guy with a lot of baggage that will just ruin your life. Daddy said I was welcome to stay in the house if I broke off the romance; otherwise, I had to leave. I moved out after a few months.

Out on my own and scouring the area for a job, I encountered all sorts of new places. There were several occasions when a new place struck me because of the interior paint color or a certain light fixture here or there. I tried to match the place to the details in my recurring dream, and each time I was able to determine that the place was not the one in my dream. The after-effects of the recurring dream hung on me like a bad stink. However, instead of being frightened, I became inquisitive. I wanted to know why I couldn't remember much of my past except the dream, and why did the dream recur. As I look back on it, I can see where my preoccupation with the dream was a big cause of my distraction and inability to learn skills I would need to succeed at work. The best job I could get was as a receptionist for a small, private engineering firm.

My boyfriend was great. He made sure that I had plenty of food to eat and gas in my car. He did his best to keep my car running, but I sometimes had to go back to my father with my tail tucked under and ask him for help. He always obliged me and never asked for money or any favor. I think my folks regretted kicking me out of the house. It was a disturbing episode for all of us.

One day I went to a specialty shop to find a cushion for a small rattan love seat someone had given me. I stopped dead in my tracks when I approached the pillows. There -- very prominently displayed -- a pillow of a certain greenish color. Everything else around me vanished: the stuff, the people and the entire store. I was fixated on that single pillow. "God help me," I remember saying to myself. I just kept staring at that pillow while mentally checking the color in my recurring dream. I was stumped. For the first time, I could not say for sure that was not the color. In fact, it was the closest I had come to seeing it in real life for 20 years.

An older lady was gently holding my arm when I finally noticed she was asking me if I was okay and if she could do anything for me. I stopped thinking about the pillow and the dream and noticed that I was sweating and shaking all over. I limped over to a seat and asked for water. After a short interrogation from the lady and a sales clerk, I excused myself by saying that I forgot to take my medicine on time and needed to get home quickly. That sounded good enough to get me out of there.

My boyfriend was at the apartment when I got home. He could see that I was shook up about something and suspected that I had been in an accident. This was the perfect opportunity for me to tell him all about my secret dream and how it had haunted me my whole life, but I couldn't say the words. He was closer to me than my best friend, but I still could not tell him. No one knew, except my mother who no doubt had forgotten all about it. I was so afraid that he would think I was a freak, or making the whole thing up for attention or just lying. He made us a nice dinner, and we ended up having a very pleasant evening. Several months later when I least expected it, I had the dream again. I was convinced and relieved that the color of the pillow was not the color in my dream. I was able to go back to the store and shop for a cushion.

As I got into my mid-20's, I embraced the dream. I felt like I was alone with it. Ever present was the feeling that the place in my dream was a part of me somehow but not from my past. I believed that if the images sprang from my past or the day's events, then I should be able to recognize some detail, but there was nothing familiar about it. I wondered what had traumatized me so and will I ever know the truth?

My mother was getting so demented that she could not drive anywhere without getting lost. My father doted on her and said she was okay despite my begging him to get her some decent medical help. I mentioned earlier about my mother's comfort with psychic phenomena. Mention is a weak word to use in her case. She had some major abilities in ESP and telepathy. She became known for one of her certain abilities, and people would seek her out for a word. I figured someone out there must know what I'm going through. Mama told me many times about her experience of hearing her older brother's voice calling her in the night. This was unusual, because he was not home. He was in Germany fighting the Nazis. She got up out of bed and went over to the window, but he wasn't there. This happened two or three times about a month before her family received the telegram that her brother had been killed in action.

I started to consider psychic phenomena and how psychology or parapsychology might explain my dream and answer my questions. I thought I should try at least to see if there was any research on the subject of dreams. I knew nothing about psychology but soon discovered the writings of Dr. Sigmund Freud, Dr. Paul Chabaneix and Dr. Carl Jung. I read Sigmund Freud first since his name sounded familiar.

In his book, <u>The Interpretation of Dreams</u>, Dr. Freud determined that dreams are created by impressions we receive from the previous day, from our childhood, or from the events our waking memory classifies as "subsidiary and unnoticed." (Freud, Sigmund, <u>The Interpretation of Dreams</u>; Translated from German and Edited by James Strachey; Basic Books; 1955; pp. 187-188.) This book devotes over 200 pages to dreams, but the recurrent dream earns only a partial page.

Dr. Freud acknowledged the existence of recurring dreams even though he never had one himself. He explains that the recurrent dream is actually a dream that occurs in childhood and then reappears in adult sleep from time to time. This is based on his discussion with a colleague about that colleague's recurrent dream involving a yellow lion, which the gentleman learns as an adult that he used to play with as a child. I decided this wasn't on point with my experience since my recurring dream started in childhood and remained recurrent through adulthood.

Good Doctor Freud graciously acknowledged the work

of one of his contemporaries, Dr. Paul Chabaneix, who determined that "…dreams that recur periodically have often been observed." (*Id* at p. 212). Meaning I must have seen or been in the place some time in my life and could only recall it in my dream. Dr. Freud later examined recurrent dreams in <u>Fragment of an Analysis of a Case of Hysteria</u>. I had had enough hysteria so I decided not to explore Dr. Freud's analysis any further. I was consoled, however, in learning that Dr. Freud and many others before him embraced the phenomenon of the recurring dream. I read in <u>The Oxford Dictionary of Psychology</u> that Dr. Freud originally considered dreams as "wish fulfillments" but later suggested that they may serve a more primitive function.

I was satisfied that recurring dreams were common and delighted to learn that I was not a freak. I stopped psychology research for a time and turned my attention to the exploding popularity of the psychic community. The only psychics I had heard about were Jeanne Dixon and Uri Geller. Mr. Geller was so popular that I could not reach him in any way. I wrote to Ms. Dixon and received a letter from her staff that my inquiry was received and would be delivered to her. While I was waiting for Ms. Dixon's response, I read somewhere that my dream, although recurring, could be a nightmare or sleep terror. Nightmares differ from dreams in that the dreamer awakes emotional and vividly recalls the details of the dream. I was always upset when I woke up from the dream, so maybe the dream really was a nightmare. I don't remember reading about people who had experienced recurring nightmares, although I suspected someone was out there somewhere. I never received an answer from Ms. Dixon and thus ended my pursuit of psychics.

There was a very popular hypnotist at the time that I thought about seeing. I don't remember her name, but she was on TV and featured in Las Vegas a lot. She was a striking, bold-speaking blond with beautiful clothes and a real talent for "hypnosis as entertainment." I decided she was probably the only person who could guide me to the meaning of my dream, but it was impossible to reach her.

I returned to my own research and came across a statement that my type of dream could be something called creative dreaming. Unfortunately, I did not write down the citation so I am unable to give credit where it is so well deserved. This led me to the names of psychologists and psychiatrists who were conducting research and providing dream therapy. None were in my area of the state, and I didn't have the money to travel to their offices. I did not find any published report on any particular research or therapy, so my only alternative would have been to seek one-on-one therapy myself. I refused to do it based foremost on the state of my economics and the confidence that I did not need a doctor. You see, I would have to tell the doctor about the dream; I couldn't do that. I thought about hypnosis, but then I might expose my early humiliations. I couldn't do that either.

I stumbled upon some of Dr. Carl G. Jung's papers on dreams. Dr. Jung agreed with Dr. Freud to the extent that dreams consist of the residue of the images or events from the day or days past. However, Dr. Jung believed that recurring dreams in childhood are often previewing our destiny. In "Approaching the Unconscious", Part 1 of <u>Man and His Symbols</u>, (Doubleday & Company, 1964, p. 40), Dr. Jung explains:

"The recurring dream is a noteworthy phenomenon. There are cases in which people have dreamed the same dream into the later years of adult life. A dream of this kind is usually an attempt to compensate for a particular defect in the dreamer's attitude to life; or it may date from a traumatic moment that has left behind some specific prejudice. <u>It may also anticipate a future event of importance</u>." (Emphasis added.)

This was my "ah hah!" moment. Since the dream didn't reveal any event from my past or present, the secret must lie in the future.

This revelation led me to find out if anyone had recorded a recurring dream that came to fruition in the future. I found only one recorded incidence. We only had libraries then, no such thing as the Internet. The only writing we (the librarian and I) could find was a description contained in the

Bible. Joseph, the son of Jacob, dreamed several dreams as a child about his destiny. While the details of his recurring dreams were graphically different, the basic theme remained the same in each dream and came to fruition 30 years later. My case was monumentally different in the most obvious sense that I'm not a prophet nor have I ever considered myself in a positive sense or wanted to elevate myself in any way. More distinctly, the details in my dreams were exactly the same each time. Another distinction is that the details in Joseph's dream were clearly visible to him. My dream was always obscure, distorted and cloaked in a foggy vagueness. Joseph's dream revealed a purpose and a blessing. My dream revealed nothing, always left me terrified and, thus, was nothing more than a curse to me.

After reading Joseph's story I continued reading the rest of the stories in the Old Testament. I liked it. I decided to read the Bible again except I started from the beginning. I still liked it, and I discovered that I wanted to know more. I started going to a new church called Calvary Chapel. The meetings were held in a big tent in Costa Mesa, and the pastor was Chuck Smith. I liked Pastor Smith's style of teaching the Bible in sequential order; and he explained everything as we went along, jumping over to cross-references only where necessary, which was a helpful way for me to learn. I learned so much after reading both the Old and New Testaments word for word without skipping around. He didn't spend

40 minutes a week preaching on little snippets of text, nor did he use his platform to conduct group therapy sessions or political rallies. I felt like I was in the right place at the right time doing the right thing for myself.

I decided to believe it is possible that God talks to people face-to-face and through dreams and visions. I had a little bit of hope in something bigger than myself, that maybe God was using the dream to speak to me personally. I would have preferred the dream to be glorious and artistic, but I was thrilled that the dream led me to the Lord and made me want to know more about Him and have a relationship with Him.

It is clear throughout the Bible that God condemns astrology, using mediums to talk to the dead and soothsayers (see Leviticus 19:31 and 20:27; Deuteronomy 4:19; and Jeremiah 8:1-3). I was glad that I didn't get all boiled up in the psychic trend. I felt that if I had, I would have done something that God tells us not to do. God wants us to lean on Him and put our faith in Him alone. The Bible says that God does not change; He is the same yesterday, today and tomorrow. (Hebrews 13:8) This is good news! Through my belief in God's promises, I was at peace with a recurring dream and happy to be in God's hands.

I read another circumstance in the Bible where God spoke to a man in a night dream. The story is about Abraham and Sarah and what happened when they stopped at a city called Gerar on their journey south toward Egypt. (Genesis 20:1-18) Abimelech, the king of Gerar, took Sarah from Abraham for his harem since Abraham, to save his own life, claimed Sarah was his sister and not his wife. But God spoke to Abimelech in a dream and told him that He would kill him if he touched Sarah. The king restored Sarah to Abraham. This story reminded me of an episode that happened when I was about 10 years old.

I was playing in the street with the other kids from the block. A young lady drove up in a car and asked how to get to a certain street in our neighborhood. It was a hard street to find because it was nestled in a small block within a block inside a large block. All of us kept pointing and shouting down each other as to the best way to get there. She said that was kind of hard to remember and asked if one of us could take her there. Instant silence. We had all been taught not to get in a car with a stranger. She seemed nice to me though. I remember thinking she was older than my sister but not as old as my mother and had pretty, blond hair. She reminded me of Elizabeth Montgomery from "Bewitched." The car was older but clean, and I remember the light blue and white paint because it looked so much like the gas tank on my brother's motorcycle.

I shot up my hand and volunteered to take her, and she opened the door for me. All the kids were screaming, "No! No! Katie, don't, don't! Get out!" I could still hear them calling out to me as we turned the corner at the end of the street. She followed my directions, but she didn't make an important right turn when I told her to. I asked her why she didn't turn. She just kept going straight. I told her she was going to have to double-back since there was no way to get to the street the way she was going. She just stared straight ahead and didn't say a word. I sat there looking at her as panic was starting to wash over me. I was struck by the sense she was negotiating whether to keep driving or take me back. I don't know exactly what she was thinking but I imagine it was something to the effect that more than one witness could describe her, the car and probably provide a license number.

As I turned away from her to decide when to jump out, I noticed another sensation in that car. It was a magical sensation. The atmosphere became very heavy, and I sensed that she decided I was not to be harmed. At the same moment she said, "Oh, I remember now how to get there. Let me take you back." She drove me right back to my street. All of the kids remained on the spot, anxiously waiting to see if they should tell my mother or call the police. They all came running with big smiles and laughter when they saw the car. I got out, and she drove away. Everybody asked me if I was scared, and I admitted that I wasn't at first but then I started to panic when she didn't follow my directions.

The older boys said I was a very lucky little girl. No one, including me, ever told my parents about what happened.

I have wondered often about that time when I was in the car with the lady and she kept staring straight and the air in that car got so thick. I wonder if God impressed upon her that I was not to be harmed. I'll never know for sure this side of heaven, but I do know that God was with me in that car that day.

4 – The Dream Revealed

I know that the root cause of all of my interpersonal failures was my emotional dysfunction. My poor boyfriend. We fought all the time over the stupidest things. I would not back down no matter how wrong I was. It was essential that I win to maintain my false sense of self-esteem. After five years of fighting, breaking up and getting back together, we married and moved about 45 miles away from our childhood homes. Many years passed and lots of turmoil from my parents over my choice of spouse, but after five or six years my parents lost their hearts to my husband. He could do no wrong. In fact, they always took his side in a dispute. My mother would say, "Obviously it's your fault; you're not doing something right."

Mama kept getting more and more deranged. We

couldn't be on the phone for more than five minutes before we started yelling at each other. She kept telling me what all I was doing wrong as a wife and homemaker, and me arguing back in defense. Our phone fights could go on for hours, yet our deep love and bond never failed. I cut down the phone calls to once a week, then once a month. I made sure to get together with my parents for special occasions and holidays, but I couldn't take too much of my mother.

One day I suddenly realized that I hadn't had the recurring dream for quite some time. In fact, I couldn't remember the last time I had had it. My life was at peace, and the recurring dream faded into the background of forgetfulness or so I thought.

I was about to turn 30. I don't know why I put so much emphasis on that age. The months, weeks and days prior to the big birthday were generally much of the same; work, eat and sleep with a few trips to the river here and there. On a certain night I had dinner and got ready for bed just like any other night. Everything with my husband was cool, and we were dog-tired. I had the dream that night. I shot up in bed. I must have uttered something to cause my husband to wake up so quickly. He kept asking if I was okay. I told him I had a nightmare. He asked what I dreamed about, and I lied to him about being chased by somebody. We never talked about it again.

I had two unsuccessful pregnancies over the years. For

consolation prizes, I acquired a couple of dogs and two cats. My little furry-faced family comforted me and kept me busy. We worked all the time trying to keep up with the house note and the rest of our bills. My father-in-law suffered a heart attack, and my mother-in-law passed away suddenly. We endured other family trauma including my brother-in-law's senseless murder in 1994. We carried on like people are supposed to do.

I remember when Daddy called me to tell me about my mother's diagnosis of advanced Alzheimer's disease in 1995. I guess he finally decided she was sicker than he had originally thought. He was crying and kept saying, "I'm so sorry, I'm so sorry." I asked him if anything could be done to help her. I knew a cure was impossible, but I still held out hope. She was beyond any advanced help, so she was left adrift without any beneficial medications or significant therapy. I sat motionless for a while after I hung up the phone. That certainly explained her. I felt horrible about how I had treated her on certain occasions. I felt guilty as though I had kicked little child or small animal. I knew my father needed me now; he needed my strength.

Mama lost the use of her left leg. Daddy bought her a walker, but she couldn't understand how to use it and kept going around in a circle. The doctor was kind enough to order a wheelchair for her. She could no longer drive, of course, but she did have a good bit of vocabulary left.

I could still get her to laugh. She soon started to stiffen up a bit and shortly became unable to feed herself. Daddy mentioned that she had choked on her food on more than one occasion. We talked about getting a nurse to help, but Daddy insisted that he was going to take care of her himself. "I don't want anybody messing with her," is how he put it. I spent every Saturday at their house baby-sitting Mama so Daddy could have a day to himself. He never stayed out longer than necessary to do the marketing, pick up medications, get a haircut, or any other small chore. I would massage Mama's hands and feet, then polish her toes and fingernails. The three of us would have supper together, and we tried hard to make a pleasant afternoon of it for her sake. We took turns feeding her and wiping her face.

Daddy was having so much trouble pushing her wheelchair through the 30-year old shag carpet. One day he just tore every bit of it out of the house. He didn't tell me he was going to do it, so naturally I was shocked the first time I saw it. It was in the Spring of 1996. I told Daddy that I noticed Mama wasn't talking much anymore and coughing too much. Daddy told me that she was starting to choke regularly on her food and he had to call the paramedics a couple of times that week. I told him he had to take her to the doctor. I went with them to the appointment.

The doctor said that she was aspirating and she had pneumonia. He told us he needed to start her on antibiotics right away and insert a G-tube into her stomach. He assured us that she would never be able to eat again through her mouth but would get plenty of nourishment and all her medications though the tube. I looked at Mama. She expressed calm panic. She understood.

I reminded my father and the doctor of my mother's living will which she made years before and which I witnessed her signing. She did not want a G-tube or antibiotics if she was in a terminal condition. She told me countless times that she never wanted to lay in a bed forever. I demanded whether the doctor agreed that a first year medical student might diagnose my mother's condition as terminal. He agreed and added that even though there was no cure or hope for her, the G-tube would make her end of life more comfortable since he did not feel her death was imminent. I asked him to define imminent, and he replied,

"Your mother could live another year or two or die tonight in her sleep. I don't know for sure, but I do know that either way she will be more comfortable."

"More comfortable while she's laying in a bed?", I fired back at him.

"Yes," said the doctor adding, "She cannot sit up or walk on her own and will finish her days in bed. Your father is her power of attorney. It is really up to him now."

The doctor excused himself by saying that he needed to

order the antibiotics and give my father and me a chance to discuss the G-tube option.

We discussed it -- for about four hours at mother's bedside. I was in an adversarial position fighting with my father to defend my mother's right to die the way she had expressed years and years before she ever showed any signs of a terminal illness. The thought of lying helpless in a bed horrified her when she was in her right mind. I kept reminding him of her living will, shouting that he must do the right thing, follow her wishes, and abide by the law.

At the end of the argument, we agreed no G-tube and no antibiotics. Mother was holding her chin up in a victorious manner and gave me a little sigh when I kissed her "goodnight until tomorrow." My father was not happy or mad or sad. He was numb. I went home fully satisfied that my mother would be started on morphine that night and that she would be comfortable as she was allowed to pass away at the hospital.

I walked into my mother's room the next morning at 9:03 a.m. To my horror, the doctor was checking mother's G-tube he had just inserted a couple hours earlier. I hit the roof screaming at both the doctor and my father. Daddy pointed toward the doctor and screamed, "He said I had to do it or she would die." That poor little woman; so much for her living will and last wishes. The doctor sent her home with hospice. He explained that in her delicate condition and under the circumstances he didn't expect her to last much longer and that pneumonia would most likely be her end within a few months. I thought, "Comforting words indeed you greedy bastard." Daddy had the hospice bed set up in the living room and that became "their room."

Over the next year my mother had three more bouts of pneumonia. My father battled each one successfully. I was there every Saturday to support my father and try to comfort Mama. My husband came with me when he could, but towards the end she had deteriorated so much that he couldn't handle it at all. She got to the point where she didn't look like a human being. She was just a collection of bones covered with a little flesh. The flesh on her back had worn off to where both of her hipbones and her tailbone were exposed. Her jaw was frozen open and her tongue had shriveled up, just like her body.

Daddy kept himself busy as mother melted away. He had a construction dumpster delivered out front to dispose of all the carpet which had been heaped up in a pile in the backyard. He spent a little time here and there painting when he wasn't busy throwing out junk. The dining room furniture was cleared out along with all the rest of the tables, sofas and chairs. The only lights in the room were the torchère behind Daddy's recliner and the 40-year old light fixture on the wall in the dining area. He kept Mama's family Bible stand next to her bed and used it as a worktable for her medications and feedings. The closets were packed, and the back bedroom had become a sanctuary for the boxes of clutter Daddy couldn't or wouldn't address. He kept two recliners, one small end table, the television and the stereo. He played the same praise and worship music over and over everyday. At a certain time in the afternoon, he would tune into the "oldies but goodies" station so they could enjoy the big band music before supper.

The nurse advised us that the end would be soon. This was so funny because she had been saying the same thing for 14 months. On a sunny Saturday afternoon in September my husband granted my request and agreed to carry Mama outside to sit in the sun for the last time. I carried her urine bag and made sure the catheter remained untangled. He held her gently in his arms while we sat in the front yard. She knew she was outside and closed her eyes. We sat there silently listening to the birds and the leaves blowing in the breeze. Daddy stayed in the house. Mama opened her eyes about ten to 15 minutes later. We decided to take her back inside, because we were afraid the breeze was too much for her.

When we got back inside, I noticed that her countenance had changed significantly. Her expression before was always wide-eyed, and she always formed her mouth into little "o" shapes as if she was trying to talk or asking a question. But after we got back in the house, her mouth was closed and she had a steely look in her eyes. I hesitate to say this but she looked as though she had been asking, begging, praying all the time over the last year to go outside one last time before she died. Now she seemed grateful and peaceful that she got to go outside. At first I thought she closed her eyes to shield them from the sun; but afterwards, I had the unshakeable sensation that she had prayed to God to thank him for letting her feel the sun again.

My husband felt the same way and was pretty shook up about it. I had to send him home to get him away from me. People always said I was very tough and could handle anything, but I could not handle my husband's tears. I noticed that I felt pretty numb inside. I remember thinking to myself, "This is a pretty heavy moment. I should be crying or shaking or something," but there was nothing. This is how it was with me. The men were crying in the background, yet I remained calm. I was even offended at their conduct and felt they should have handled it better as men.

A few weeks after we took her outside, Mama's body stopped accepting food. This was the 19th day of October. The hospice nurse was so kind and relieved when she told me that my mother would probably die within a few days due to her ravaged state. We held hands as we prayed and thanked God for His mercy and comfort in knowing that she was going to be with Him very soon.

A week went by, and my mother didn't die. I kept

questioning the nurse about it (harassing her is probably more accurate). She told us that some people have very strong hearts, and that it takes a while for the body to break down badly enough to stop the heart. The nurse noted that the amount of fluid was remarkably low in the urine bag, so she deduced that the kidneys were "failing nicely", that it was just a matter of days if not hours; and no matter how we felt about it, "my mother was going to die on the day and at the moment and in the manner which God ordained."

Another week went by, and my mother didn't die. My father assured me that he told the doctor what was going on, and the doctor agreed with the nurse -- that mother would die very soon of a heart attack caused by starvation.

Another week went by. My mother was still alive, sort of. Her breath was remarkably shallow even from the days prior. I opened her eyelids and saw that her eyes were starting to get cloudy like a dead fish. I went atomic. I screamed at my father. I called the nurse, and I screamed at her. Daddy went outside for I don't know how long, long enough for me to stop screaming at him from inside the house. He had never seen me that mad and that hysterical at the same time. It scared him enough to call the doctor to find out what to do about me; he asked the doctor what pill prescribed to my mother could he give me to shut me up.

I heard the doctor yell, "She's not dead yet?" I could hear my father defending himself to the doctor that he was not feeding her anything. The doctor asked if she was still getting her medications, and Daddy admitted that he was still giving her prescriptions regularly with water even though he had been told by the doctor and nurses weeks ago to stop. The doctor simply said, "You must for her sake stop all fluids, nothing goes in her G-tube whatsoever!" All he should have been giving her was the morphine under her tongue. Daddy hung up and collapsed. He truly believed that he was going to be responsible for killing her. The doctor must have called the nurse, because she showed up within minutes.

The nurse got my father in an altered state so we could get him off the floor and into a chair, then we turned our attention back to my mother. The nurse said she had never heard of anything like it, and that none of her colleagues believed her when she discussed us at their weekly case meetings. She said that mother was alive because Daddy kept giving her water regularly. She informed me that a healthy person might live two to four weeks without water depending on their physical condition, but generally a person could die in a week without water, especially someone in mother's condition. This was on Sunday, the second day of November.

I spent the next four days at work expecting my father to be at the other end of every phone call, but he didn't call me at all. I called countless times during the day each day and talked to him or the nurse, and each day the response was the same: "no change"; "she's hanging in there"; "it should be any moment now." I remember driving home one night screaming hysterically, crying out to God all the way. Drivers flashed their lights and tried to flag me over, but no one could reach me. I was traumatized. Why, God? Why? How was it possible for this poor woman not to have any food for two weeks and then go without food and water in her condition and still be alive?

I went to the house as usual on Saturday, November 7, on what turned out to be the seventh day she had no water. There was "something in the air" as soon as I walked into the house. Immediately I suspected Daddy and accused him of giving her water again. Then I accused him of torturing her. The argument was escalating quickly, so he decided it was a good time for him to run his errands. I screamed to him on his way out, "You wouldn't let an animal suffer like this!" I sat down in the chair next to mother and leaned over to pet her head.

Daddy taught me how to shoot a gun and took me to target practice a lot when I was growing up. I knew exactly where he kept his .22 pistol. I had to kill her. I thought of how to shoot her and about the consequences. I wasn't concerned about prison or ruining my life, but I did worry about how to muffle the shot. As I straightened up in the chair, the large bottle of morphine on the Bible stand next to the bed caught my eye. I remember thinking this was perfect. She was full of morphine already, we were waiting for death at any moment, meaning there would be no autopsy, and so I could probably get away with it. I held the bottle in my hand while I decided whether to pour it down her throat all at once or just squeeze it in her mouth with the dropper however many times it took to use it all up. I decided the right thing to do was to pour the liquid down her throat a little at a time. I reached through the bed guard and gently laid my hand on her forearm. I just wanted to touch her warm body one last time in love. As I got up to kiss her and initiate my plan I noticed, there above my head, but just off to the right, *the light*.

The light from my dream! I started crying so hard and could barely get out the words "Oh my God!" I knew instantly that I was in the middle of my recurring dream as it was unfolding to my natural eyes. First, always first, was the light. The light, I finally saw the light for what it was. It was the dining room light on the wall. It should have been brighter because it was a two-light fixture, but one of the light bulbs had blown out. I knew exactly what was going to happen next. I was sobbing and shaking. I knew the green color was coming. I looked to the left just like I had always dreamed and then I knew what the green color was. It was the green paint on the walls throughout the whole house. All of my life I couldn't decipher the color because the walls that were avocado-green for so long had been painted over white. Thirty-four years of being haunted by a hideous green color were evaporating.

I continued to pan my gaze to the left around the room as always occurred in the dream. There were the windows. Starting with the back door which consisted of two large pieces of sliding glass, then a corner structure, then four fixed windows separated by metal strips which made up picture windows on the south wall. These were the six big windows in my dream. Then I recognized the smell.

The smell is the hardest aspect of the dream to describe especially because it is not just one smell as I had thought for so many years. It turned out to be a mixture of several different odors. One of the smells was the pungent smell from the perineal foam skin cleanser, add to that the heavy sweet smell from the medicated skin cream, then mix in the stench of decaying flesh. To top it off, Daddy had put on a pot of pinto beans that morning, and the smell of cooked beans was wafting through the house. All those smells mixed together into one noxious note.

Next came the sound. Finally, the weird humming

sound was revealed. What I thought was one sound in my dream was actually from two machines. These machines were running non-stop in the room. There was a compressor over in the corner for oxygen but it also pumped air into the pressure-point mattress pad on the bed. The pad consisted of baffles that floated up and down when air flowed from one baffle to another from head to toe and back again. When the machine was "on" to pump air, the motor kicked up to a higher speed and made a higher pitched sound. When the head-to-toe cycle was completed, the motor kicked down to a resting, continuous hum. There was a HEPA-filter fan between my mother's bed and the day bed we brought over for Daddy to sleep on. This fan also ran continuously at a dull nag rather than a hum.

Layer-by-layer I was coming to terms with the details of the dream. I kept looking around, but I never saw the black curtain or anything dark. I could see clearly down the hallway that separated the master bedroom from my old room. The hall was well lit, and I could see all of the doors and the doorknobs on the cupboards at the end of the hall. I remember asking myself where was the black? Then I looked down. I could see! There was no black. I looked down just like I did in the dream to see that pitiful, tortured remain of a once vibrant and wonderful woman -- that pathetic and hideous sight. Not just that it was my mother, but the condition of the body and the fact that it was another human being made it especially horrifying. The black represented death.

ର୨ରଇ

I put down the bottle of morphine. I didn't kill my mother as I fully intended to do. God stopped me. When I was five years old, He gave me a vision of this place, this time and this circumstance. As the vision became reality before my eyes, I knew that God chose that moment in the past to stop me in the future. My dream contained no illustrious acts or pomp and circumstance, no great elevation to a higher position in life, no hidden treasure or untold glory. It was a gift from God outside of my space and time to shock me into reality and stop me from murdering my mother. In the midst of this revelation, an amazing, indescribable feeling overwhelmed me. I felt like I had been dropped from a high place into a giant lake made from three deep pools: the pool of grief, the pool of confusion and the pool of comfort.

The pool of grief consisted of all the emotions that naturally occur with the loss of a loved one. Deep sadness was the primary emotion in this pool. My mother was dying, tortured slowly in front of my eyes for more than a year. I was so sad, and I was helpless to do anything to save her. My helplessness gave birth to a deep anxiety, and the anxiety brought forth guilt. The guilt was compounded as I continued to ponder the dream and its truth. I kept telling myself that I should have been able to stop it or make it better for her somehow, because I knew so much of the situation in advance but yet I didn't know what it was. This is how it was in the pool of confusion.

In the pool of confusion were all of the details of the recurring dream without any clarity concerning the key components. The key components were always concealed by undetectable layers: the fact that the place turned out to be my childhood home; that my mother lay dying was the black, the dark place that I could never see; that my mother was in such a horrible, emaciated state. No one should ever have to see a loved one in that condition. I had seen plenty of dying relatives and none were so ravaged. I kept asking myself why was I cursed with this vague dream that held no value of any kind for so long. The dream was a jumble of unanswered questions wrapped up in a conundrum. What purpose did it serve?

At this point I felt the rush from the water in the pool of comfort. I remembered the story of Joseph and his dream, and how he had waited 30 years for his dream to be fulfilled. I realized that I was not cursed, but God blessed me with the dream as a gift to help me in the crucible of my circumstance.

I was amazed that God gave me such a gift. God knows me -- me -- the individual, not just another female in a vast sea full of billions of other females. And He cares for me. I had to face the truth that God stopped me when I was five from committing a murder at 39. God became very real to me at that moment.

I knew I had to pull myself together rather quickly since my father would be coming home. I stroked Mama's head for a little while and prayed over her. I thanked God for all His mercies to my family and to me, and I thanked Him for bringing comfort to me in a mighty and powerful way. Mama sighed. This Saturday visit would be the last Saturday I would spend with her. She died the following Wednesday, and we buried her on Friday. She had lain in that hospice bed for a total of 16 months and eleven days.

5 – The Dream's Purpose

Just the family attended the funeral. The pastor we invited told our congregation later that we comforted him rather than the other way around simply because we personified the confidence we believed that our wife and mother was in the presence of the Lord. Sure we were sad, but we were so happy that her suffering was over. No more tears, no more pain; we rejoiced in God's promises, confident that she is with Him.

"So we are always confident, knowing that while we are at home in the body we are absent from the Lord. For we walk by faith, not by sight. We are confident, yes, well pleased rather to be absent from the body and to be present with the Lord." (2 Corinthians 5:6-8)

The hours between Mama's death and her funeral are a

blur. I was so distracted with my heavy secrets that I forgot to arrange a ride to the funeral for my brother. I didn't even think about him until we had been home from the cemetery for a couple of hours and I was alerted that my brother was on the phone asking when I was going to pick him up. I could hardly speak to him; I was so mortified and hurt that I had forgotten all about him. He handled it well on the phone, but I know he was devastated. I didn't offer him any excuses, because I knew he wouldn't believe me no matter what I said. I told him the truth that I completely forgot about him and never intended to hurt him. Who forgets to take her own brother to his mother's funeral?

I was very unsettled for months after the funeral. I was restless. I snapped at everyone and barked at my husband. I had to tell him about the dream and what I had done. I kept thinking how is it possible that I could have lived in that house, walked in and out of it everyday for almost 20 years and never caught a glimpse of the signposts all around me, especially the last year and a half that mother was in hospice. It is preposterous and defied my ability to reason. I finally settled on the answer that was to be found in the dream itself. The details were clear enough to give me a signal but clouded and shadowy enough so that the signal was not clear -- like looking at something through a glass bottle. I was so committed and determined to end my mother's suffering that only God could have stopped me. There is no other explanation; it had to be God that gave me the dream.

I finally decided to tell my best friend, my husband, about this great gift I had received from the Lord. I couldn't wait for him to stop watching the television. He was a little ticked off that I insisted on interrupting his game, but when I started to cry he knew it was serious and gave me his undivided attention. I did real well in the telling of the story until I had to explain the day the dream was revealed. My heart and spirit were shaken with every detail, and I was shivering as I peeled back each layer of the dream. It was altogether so real and wondrous and scary and comforting. I was ashamed as I told him about the morphine and what I was going to do with it.

My husband wept with me and held me in his arms as he told me how much he loves me. He wanted to know if there was anything he could do for me -- a glass of wine, a sedative, a straightjacket? We laughed and marveled at what we believed it all meant. He said I had to tell other people about the dream and what the Lord did for me.

I dug deep into my Bible study. When I got back into the New Testament again, I was shaken by the story of the demon-possessed man who lived among the tombs in the land of the Gadarenes. Jesus commanded the unclean spirit to depart from the man, and he was made whole and in his right mind. The man was so grateful and begged Jesus to take him with him, but Jesus didn't allow it. Instead, Jesus said to the man,

"Go home to your friends, and tell them what great things the Lord has done for you, and how He has had compassion on you." (Mark 5:1-20)

From this I determined that my husband's advice was wise and true. God did not curse me with a haunting dream but blessed me with a recurring dream that I could share with others to help them and perhaps guide them to consider the truths contained in God's word. I was fully persuaded that I had not dreamed a dream but I was given a vision. I believe that the vision was a gift from God to help me confirm my faith in Him. Because God gave me the dream at such a young age, I know with complete certainty that He is aware of all the bad things that I would ever think, say or do before I was ever born, and yet He still blessed me with His special touch, a secret gift between Him and me, to let me know that He knows I am alive and that He values me and gave His life for me. What other possible response could I have other than to return such love, mercy and grace with complete confidence, obedience and love.

"We love Him because He first loved us." (1 John 4:19)

I reviewed my life and all the ways that the Lord intervened. I am proud to stand with the Lord and obey his commandments. I know that on this side of heaven that it is impossible to be perfect, so to please God I must put my faith in Jesus' death on the cross. He died for me to save me so I could be reconciled with God and live with Him in heaven forever along with my departed loved ones who also believed.

One day in the middle of my work it dawned on me that I hadn't dreamed the dream in a seriously long time. I had to stop work and figure out the dates. It had been a little over five years since my mother died. I started to laugh, a loud laugh of joy and relief. A couple of curious coworkers popped over to ask what was so funny. I couldn't tell them, so I lied. I recalled a recent conversation with a friend who described the blackmail she would use on her little boy if he dared to become a troubled teen. Everyone laughed and went about their work as I sat amazed.

I thought of all those years, all that trauma and dysfunction, all the emotional wrangling now stopped. I examined my thoughts and determined that not only had no fear of the dream occurred to me since I confided in my husband, but I also felt no sense of loss by not dreaming the dream. My conscience was a peace, and the years past without fear. Isn't that what the Lord tells us?

"Be strong and courageous. Do not be afraid or terrified because of them, for the Lord your God goes with you; he will never leave you nor forsake you." (Deuteronomy 31:6)

"But now, this is what the LORD says— he who created you, O Jacob, he who formed you, O Israel: "Fear not, for I

*have redeemed you; I have summoned you by name; you are mine." (*Isaiah 43:1)

"*Indeed, the very hairs of your head are numbered. Don't be afraid; you are worth more than many sparrows." (*Luke 12:7)

"And surely I am with you always, to the very end of the age." (Matthew 28:20)

These are just a few of the dozens of times that God tells us not to be afraid because He is with us. Isn't this why we check our horoscope or go to palm readers or psychic mediums? We want to know the future so we won't be afraid. I lived in constant fear for so long. I never knew when the proverbial "other shoe was going to drop", and I suffered emotional and physical setbacks as a result. But God in His Grace revealed His truth to me through His Word and set me in a place where I can say, "Blessed assurance, Jesus is mine" (based on Hebrews 10:22; from the song "Assurance", lyrics by Fanny Crosby, music by Phoebe Knapp). God didn't curse me with a horror; He gave me an experience so that I could declare with all confidence to others that He is alive and working in all of our lives. If He weren't, there would be no "déjà vu" term because there would be no déjà vu moments. I can say like Job:

"Though He slay me, yet will I hope in Him; I will surely defend my ways to His face." (Job 13:15)

It has been over 13 years now since the dream was

revealed, and I still rejoice in the experience. I haven't had the dream again, so I know for certain that it was not a fluke and was in fact a glimpse into a certain event in my life, my destiny. Even though it was horrible while it lasted, it turned out to be a blessing of the highest order. I have so many more stories and tons of details to share about extraordinary and horrifying events that I endured on my faith journey, but as I was writing it all sounded like "blah, blah, blah, blah, blah, blah, blah." It isn't necessary to suffocate you with mountainous details just to fill a page. It is important, however, to focus on the main reason for my revealing this story. It is, as I said, to tell you what God has done for me. Perhaps you had a wonderful life with little to no hassle and a great future. Maybe you also had a recurring dream, or vision, or glimpse at your destiny. There is room for me to believe that I am not alone in my experience.

If you have had some sort of paranormal event, I hope that my story will lead you to the Bible for your answers. I refuse to accept that we are more than 4,500 years removed from the giving of the law by God through Moses with no hope that scriptural principles and truths have no application to our everyday lives whatsoever. It happened to me, and I believe it has or will happen to you.

"I was blind but now I see!" (John 9:25)

This is the heartbeat of my story. I struggled for 34 years

with a mystery that clouded my mind with terror and apprehension; but now I see clearly. I can face my demons. More importantly, I can forgive the men and women that hurt me intentionally and unintentionally. Because I know that the Lord is faithful and true, I can place my unknown future in the hands of a God that I know. And I know who He is because He has revealed Himself in His Word. He tells me:

He knows my name

"Before I was born, the Lord called me; from my birth he has made mention of my name." (Isaiah 49:1)

He guides my steps

"*He guides me in the paths of righteousness for his name's sake.*" (Ps 23:3)

He knew me before I was born

"This is what the LORD says— your Redeemer, who formed you in the womb: I am the LORD, who has made all things, who alone stretched out the heavens, who spread out the earth by myself, …" (Isaiah 44:24)

He thinks about me

"What is man that you are mindful of him?" (Ps 8:4)

He knows my thoughts before I think them

"Before a word is on my tongue you, Lord, know it completely." (Ps 139:4)

He forgives my sin

"For God so loved the world that He gave His one and only Son, that whoever believes in Him shall not perish but have eternal life." (John 3:16)

He forgets my sin

"I, even I, am he who blots out your transgressions, for my own sake, and remembers your sin no more." (Isaiah 43:25)

I can smile at the sunrise, because I am reminded each morning that His mercies are new everyday. (Lamentations 3:22-23). Yet the most important evidence of His love is His sacrifice at the cross, the highest expression of love.

"Greater love hath no man than this, that a man lay down his life for his friends." (John 15:13)

I hope you will not be lulled into a heretical theory that if you accept the free gift of salvation that you can think, say and do whatever you want without consequence. By no means! God's grace is not to be applied and discarded at will. If you are involved in sinful conduct, you must repent. You must stop what you are doing, turn away from it and continue no more in that direction: *"'No one, sir,' she said. 'Then neither do I condemn you,' Jesus declared. 'Go now and leave your life of sin.'"* (John 8:11, the story of the woman caught in the act of adultery).

Repentance is necessary to please God. If you are too shy

to tell others about God's grace, then the change in your behavior and attitude will cause them to ask you why you have changed thus providing you an opportunity to explain God's work in your life. We can't be perfect like God this side of heaven no matter how hard we try each and every minute of the day, but we can follow the examples of some of the people presented in the Bible: Rahab, the harlot (Joshua 2:1-16 and Hebrews 11:31); the Samaritan Woman at the Well (John 4:1-42); and the Mad Man of Gadara (Mark 5:1-20), just to name a few.

Of course, I realize how strange my story sounds. But I'm not ashamed of the gospel. I am certain God has revealed Himself to you, too, at some time in some way. Perhaps a near-miss accident at your workplace, on the highway or at home. Perhaps you just knew something bad was going to happen to someone before finding out that it had. Perhaps you know when the phone is about to ring. Some people describe themselves as lucky or say that everything they touch turns to gold. You might know in your gut when you meet someone that they cannot be trusted. No matter how small or great the detail may be, God has spoken to you. If you think He has not, then consider this: the sun comes up every morning. Everyday is an opportunity to become self-aware of your condition and His mercies. There is nothing to fear and everything to gain.

"I know that my Redeemer lives, and that in the end he will stand upon the earth. And after my skin has been destroyed, yet in my flesh I will see God; I myself will see him with my own eyes - I and not another. How my heart yearns within me!" (Job 19:25-27)

To God be all thanks, glory, honor, and praise, for to Him these accolades truly belong.

Prologue

❧

"Your Great Love"

(a song)

You were coming toward me when I saw you.
Your Spirit gently leads me.
No ancient magic incantations to tell my soul.
Your love is all that I need.
(Chorus) Hallelujah! You saw me from forever.
And you saved me, no matter what I've done.
How you love me! You fill me with your Spirit.
Until I see your face, I will tell everyone …
of your great love.
*(Bridge) I can smile at the sunrise. New mercies come from
you each day.*
(Chorus) Hallelujah! You saw me from forever.
And you saved me, no matter what I've done.
How you love me! You fill me with your Spirit.
Until I see your face, I will tell everyone …
of your great love.